This book is your go-to guide for unlocking the full power of Microsoft Word. With clear, step-by-step instructions, it walks you through everything from the basics to advanced tools, helping you create professional documents with ease.

Whether you're just starting out, looking to improve your skills, or aiming to master Word, this guide is here to support you. May it boost your creativity, enhance your productivity, and make your journey to mastering Microsoft Word simple and rewarding.

Table of Contents

Chapter 1. Introduction to Microsoft Word

Microsoft Word is a word processing application that is part of the Microsoft Office suite. It allows users to create, edit, format, and share documents with ease. Whether you are writing simple text documents, creating reports, or designing complex layouts, Word offers powerful tools to meet a wide range of needs.

Why Use Word?

- **Ease of Use**: Word's user-friendly interface makes it accessible for beginners and advanced users alike.
- **Versatile Features**: It supports a wide array of document types, from simple letters to professional reports, resumes, flyers, and more.
- **Collaboration**: Word allows you to track changes, add comments, and share documents for real-time collaboration.
- **Professional Formatting**: Word offers many formatting tools for creating polished documents, such as custom styles, templates, and rich text features.
- **Integration**: As part of the Microsoft Office suite, Word integrates well with other programs like Excel, PowerPoint, and Outlook, allowing easy sharing of data and content.

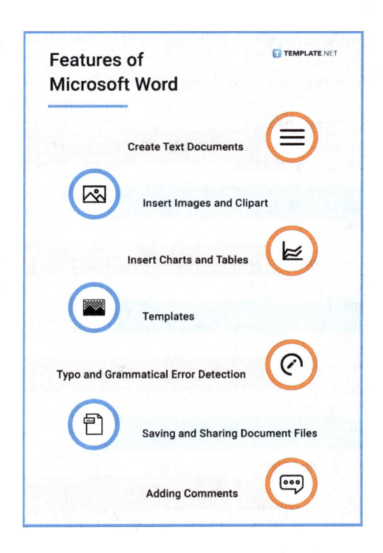

System Requirements and Installation

To use Microsoft Word, you need a compatible device with the following minimum system requirements:

- **Operating System**: Windows 10/11 or macOS (latest versions)
- **Processor**: 1.6 GHz or higher
- **RAM**: 4 GB or more
- **Hard Disk Space**: 4 GB of available disk space or more
- **Display**: 1280 x 768 screen resolution or higher
- **Internet Connection**: Required for online features, updates, and subscriptions (Microsoft 365)

Installation:

1. Purchase or subscribe to Microsoft Office or Microsoft 365.
2. Download the installation file from the official Microsoft website.
3. Follow the on-screen instructions to install Word on your device.
4. Sign in with your Microsoft account to activate your copy of Word.

Overview of the Word Interface

- **Ribbon**: The Ribbon is the main toolbar at the top of the Word window. It contains tabs like **Home**, **Insert**, **Design**, **Layout**, etc. Each tab provides a collection of related tools. For example, the **Home** tab has tools for font formatting, paragraph alignment, and styles, while the **Insert** tab lets you add tables, images, and other elements.
- **Quick Access Toolbar**: Located above the Ribbon, the Quick Access Toolbar allows you to customize and access frequently

used commands, such as **Save**, **Undo**, and **Redo**. You can add your preferred commands to this toolbar for quicker access.

- **Status Bar**: The Status Bar at the bottom of the window provides information about your document, such as page number, word count, and language. You can also adjust the document's view mode (e.g., print layout, web layout) from the Status Bar.

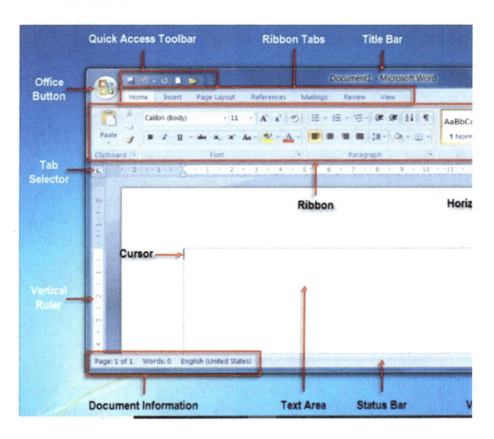

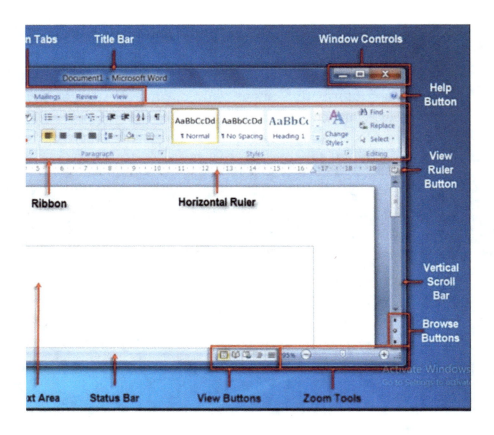

File Menu Overview (Backstage View)

The **File Menu** is accessed by clicking the **File** tab in the upper left corner of Word. This opens **Backstage View**, where you can manage your document and perform tasks such as saving, opening, and printing files.

- **Info**: Provides details about the document, such as its size, author, and word count. You can also manage document protection settings here.
- **New**: Create a new document, use a template, or access a recently used file.
- **Open**: Open an existing document from your computer, OneDrive, or other cloud storage locations.
- **Save / Save As**: Save the current document or save it with a new name or location. You can also use **Save As** to change the file format.
- **Print**: Print your document or adjust printer settings. This is where you can configure page setup and print options.
- **Share**: Share the document via email or OneDrive for collaborative editing.
- **Export**: Export the document to other formats, such as PDF.
- **Close**: Close the current document.
- **Account**: Access your Microsoft account settings and update your Office subscription.

Chapter 2. Getting Started with Word

Creating a New Document

To begin working in Microsoft Word, you'll first need to create a new document. Here's how you can do that:

1. **Opening Word**:
   - If Word is not already open, click on the **Word icon** on your desktop or start menu.
   - Once Word opens, you'll be greeted by the **Start Screen**.
2. **Creating a Blank Document**:
   - From the **Start Screen**, click on **Blank Document**. This will open a new, untitled Word document where you can start typing right away.
3. **Using a Template**:
   - Instead of a blank document, you can also use a template. Templates are pre-designed documents that provide structure and formatting, such as resumes, flyers, reports, and more.
   - To use a template, from the **Start Screen**, click on the **Search for Online Templates** box, type in what you're looking for (e.g., "resume"), and choose a template from the results.

Opening, Saving, and Closing Documents

1. **Opening Documents**:
   - To open an existing document, click on the **File** tab in the Ribbon, and then select **Open**. You will be presented with recent documents, or you can browse your computer, OneDrive, or other cloud storage locations to find the file.
   - **Shortcut**: Press **Ctrl + O** to quickly open a document.
2. **Saving Documents**:
   - To save your work, click on the **File** tab and select **Save** or use the **Save** icon in the Quick Access Toolbar.

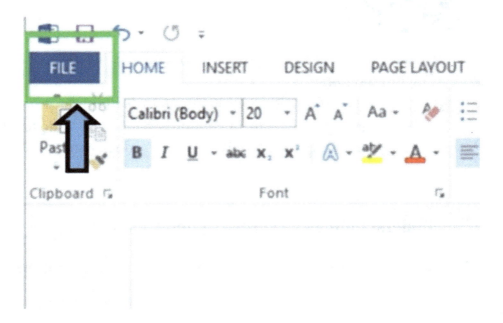

   - **Save As**: If you want to save the document under a new name or location, click on **File > Save As** and choose a different folder or filename.

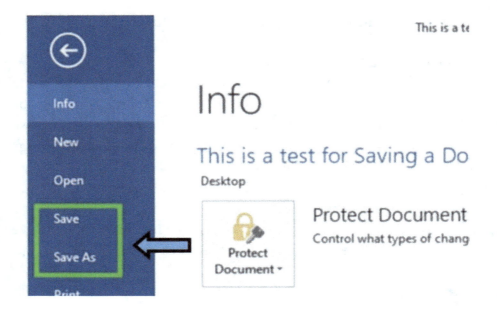

- o **Shortcut**: Press **Ctrl + S** to save your document.
3. **Closing Documents**:
   - o To close the document, click on the **X** in the upper-right corner of the document window, or go to **File > Close**.
   - o **Shortcut**: Press **Ctrl + W** to close the document.

Understanding File Formats (.docx, .dotx, .pdf)

When saving your Word document, it's essential to understand the various file formats available and when to use them:

1. **.docx (Word Document)**:
   - o This is the default file format for Word documents. It supports all Word features, including text, images, tables, and formatting.

- o **When to Use**: Use this format when working in Word and when the document needs to be edited or shared with others who use Word.
2. **.dotx (Word Template)**:
   - o A .dotx file is a template file that contains pre-designed layouts, formatting, and structure. It does not contain document content but serves as a starting point for new documents.
   - o **When to Use**: Use this format when creating templates that you want others to use as a basis for their documents.
3. **.pdf (Portable Document Format)**:
   - o PDF is a read-only file format that preserves the formatting and layout of the document, making it suitable for sharing and printing.
   - o **When to Use**: Use this format when you need to share your document with others but don't want them to be able to edit it. This is common for reports, invoices, and official forms.

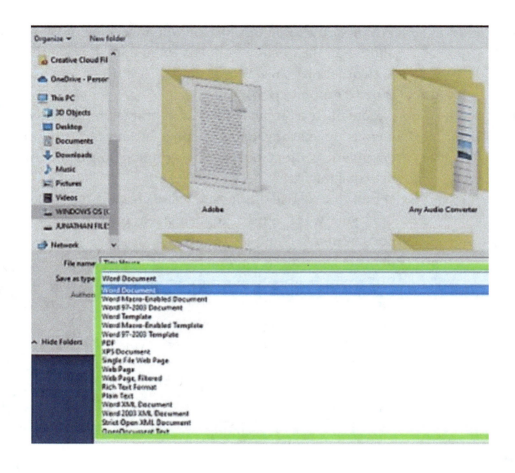

Recovering Unsaved Documents

Accidents happen, and sometimes documents are lost due to system crashes, power outages, or forgetting to save. Fortunately, Word provides ways to recover unsaved documents:

1. **AutoSave**:

- If you are using **Microsoft 365** or have **AutoSave** enabled, your document is saved automatically to OneDrive every few seconds.
- Check the **AutoSave** toggle in the upper-left corner to ensure it is turned on.

2. **Document Recovery (AutoRecovery)**:
   - If Word crashes or closes unexpectedly, it automatically attempts to recover the document the next time you open the application.
   - Upon reopening Word, look for the **Document Recovery** pane on the left side of the screen. It will display any recovered files. Click on the document you want to open.

3. **Manually Recovering an Unsaved Document**:
   - If you accidentally close a document without saving, go to **File > Info** and click on **Manage Document**.
   - Select **Recover Unsaved Documents**. Word will display a list of unsaved documents. Choose the document you want to recover.
   - Save the document immediately to avoid losing it again.

4. **Check the Temporary File Folder**:
   - In some cases, Word may save a temporary version of your document to your computer's hard drive.
   - Navigate to the **Temp Folder** on your computer (usually located in **C:\Users\YourName\AppData\Local\Temp**) and search for files with the extension **.asd** (AutoSave) or **.wbk** (backup). Open these files in Word to see if they contain the content you're missing.

Chapter 3. Basic Text Editing and Formatting

Typing, Selecting, Copying, Cutting, and Pasting Text

1. **Typing Text**:
    - Start typing directly in the document to add text. As you type, the text will appear in the location of the cursor. To move the cursor, simply click with the mouse or use the arrow keys on your keyboard.
2. **Selecting Text**:
    - **Using the Mouse**: Click and drag your mouse over the text you want to select.
    - **Using the Keyboard**: Hold down **Shift** and use the arrow keys to extend your selection.
    - **Select All**: Press **Ctrl + A** to select the entire document.
3. **Copying Text**:
    - **Using the Mouse**: Right-click on the selected text and choose **Copy** from the context menu.
    - **Using the Keyboard**: Press **Ctrl + C** to copy the selected text.
4. **Cutting Text**:
    - **Using the Mouse**: Right-click on the selected text and choose **Cut** from the context menu.

- **Using the Keyboard**: Press **Ctrl + X** to cut the selected text. This removes the text from its current location and places it on the clipboard.

5. **Pasting Text**:
   - **Using the Mouse**: Right-click on the location where you want to place the text and choose **Paste** from the context menu.
   - **Using the Keyboard**: Press **Ctrl + V** to paste the text at the cursor's location.

6. **Paste Special Options**:
   - After copying or cutting text, you can use the **Paste Special** options to control the format in which the text is pasted.
   - Go to **Home > Paste > Paste Special** to choose from options like pasting as plain text, keeping the original formatting, or other specific formats.

Formatting Fonts: Bold, Italics, Underline, and Color

1. **Bold**:
   - To make text bold, highlight the text you want to change and click on the **Bold** button in the **Font** group on the **Home** tab or press **Ctrl + B**. Bold text is useful for emphasizing important words or headings.

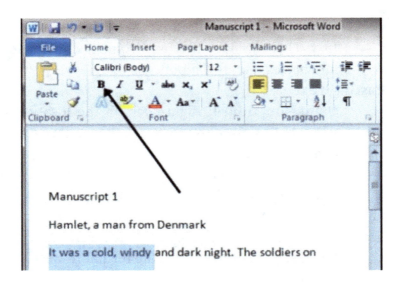

2. **Italics**:
   o To italicize text, highlight the text and click on the **Italic** button in the **Font** group on the **Home** tab or press **Ctrl + I**. Italics can be used for emphasis or to indicate titles of books, movies, or other creative works.

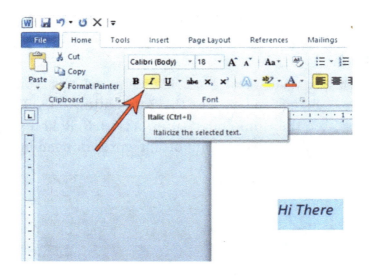

3. **Underline**:
   - o To underline text, select the text and click on the **Underline** button in the **Font** group on the **Home** tab or press **Ctrl + U**. Underlining is commonly used to highlight specific words or phrases, especially in headings.

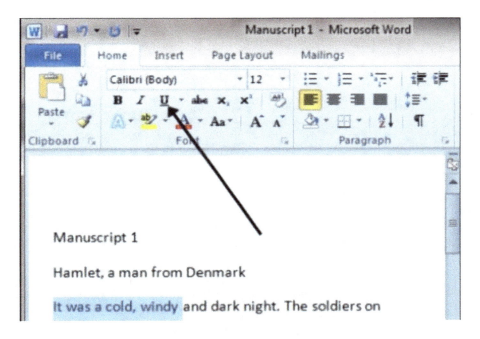

4. **Text Color**:
   - o To change the color of the text, highlight the text and click the **Font Color** button (the "A" with a color bar) in the **Font** group on the **Home** tab. Choose a color from the dropdown menu, or click **More Colors** for additional color options.

o You can also apply text color to a selection by choosing from the theme colors, standard colors, or custom colors.

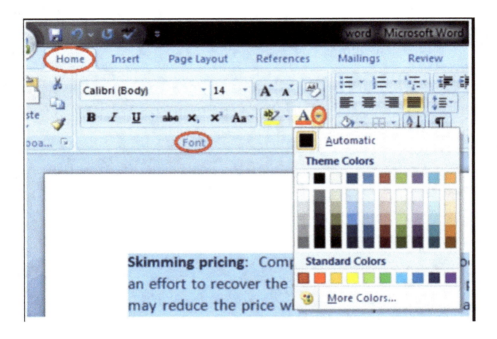

Using the Format Painter Tool

The **Format Painter** tool allows you to quickly copy formatting from one part of the document and apply it to another. It is an efficient way to maintain consistency in the formatting of your document.

1. **Using the Format Painter**:
   o Select the text that has the formatting you want to copy.
   o On the **Home** tab, click the **Format Painter** button (paintbrush icon) in the **Clipboard** group.

2. **Applying the Formatting**:
   - o   After selecting the text with the desired format, the cursor will change to a paintbrush icon. Now, highlight the text you want to apply the formatting to.
   - o   Release the mouse button to apply the formatting.
3. **Double-Click to Use Format Painter Multiple Times**:
   - o   If you need to apply the same formatting to multiple places in your document, double-click the **Format Painter** button instead of clicking once. This will keep the Format Painter tool active until you deactivate it by pressing **Esc** or clicking the button again.
4. **Clear Formatting**:
   - o   If you accidentally apply incorrect formatting, you can easily clear the formatting by selecting the text and clicking the **Clear All Formatting** button (eraser icon) in the **Font** group on the **Home** tab.

The **Format Painter** is a powerful tool for keeping the document's design consistent, especially when you want to apply styles, fonts, colors, and other text formatting to multiple sections of your document without redoing the formatting from scratch each time.

Chapter 4. Paragraph Formatting

Adjusting Line Spacing and Indents

1. **Line Spacing**:
   - **Adjust Line Spacing**: Line spacing refers to the amount of space between each line of text within a paragraph. To adjust line spacing:
     1. Select the text or paragraph you want to modify.
     2. Go to the **Home** tab, and in the **Paragraph** group, click on the **Line and Paragraph Spacing** button (icon with lines and up/down arrows).
     3. Choose from options like **1.0 (Single)**, **1.5**, **2.0 (Double)**, or click **Line Spacing Options** to fine-tune your spacing.

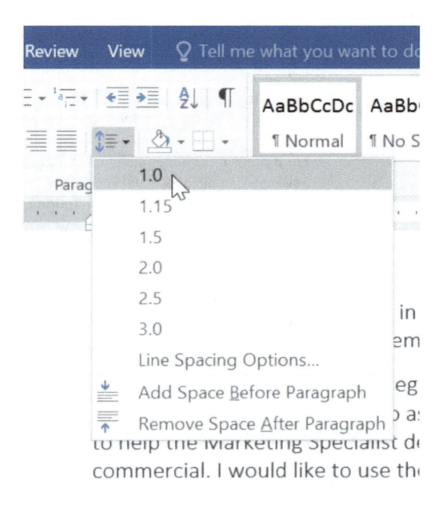

- o **Custom Line Spacing**: In the **Line Spacing Options** dialog box, you can adjust the exact spacing before and after paragraphs, as well as set specific line spacing values like **At Least**, **Exactly**, or **Multiple**.
2. **Paragraph Indentation**:
   - o **First Line Indent**: To indent only the first line of a paragraph:
     1. Select the paragraph you want to modify.

2. In the **Paragraph** group on the **Home** tab, click the **Increase Indent** or **Decrease Indent** button.
3. Alternatively, go to the **Layout** tab and adjust the **Indent** settings under the **Paragraph** section.
4. For a precise first-line indent, click **Paragraph Settings** (small arrow in the corner of the Paragraph group), and in the **Indents and Spacing** tab, set the **Special** drop-down menu to **First line** and specify the indent size.

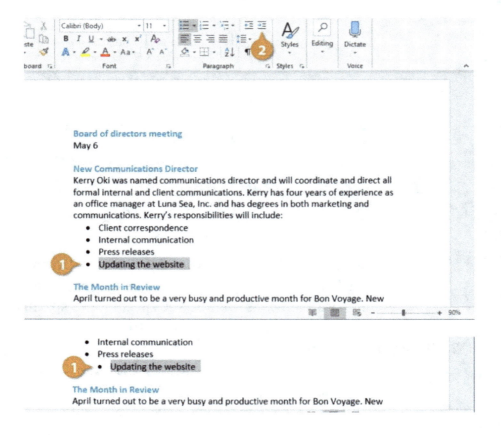

- o **Hanging Indent**: To indent all lines except the first line:
    1. Follow the steps above and choose **Hanging** from the **Special** drop-down menu in the **Paragraph Settings** dialog box.

Setting Paragraph Alignment (Left, Center, Right, Justify)

1. **Left Alignment** (default):
    - o Aligns text to the left margin and leaves the right side jagged.
    - o To align text to the left, select the paragraph and click on the **Left Align** button in the **Paragraph** group on the **Home** tab or press **Ctrl + L**.
2. **Center Alignment**:
    - o Centers the text between the left and right margins, often used for titles or headings.
    - o Select the paragraph, click the **Center Align** button in the **Paragraph** group, or press **Ctrl + E**.
3. **Right Alignment**:
    - o Aligns text to the right margin and leaves the left side jagged, typically used for dates or other right-aligned content.
    - o Select the paragraph, click the **Right Align** button in the **Paragraph** group, or press **Ctrl + R**.
4. **Justify Alignment**:
    - o Aligns text to both the left and right margins, creating a clean, straight edge on both sides, with extra spacing

between words. Commonly used for newspaper or magazine-style documents.
- o Select the paragraph, click the **Justify** button in the **Paragraph** group, or press **Ctrl + J**.

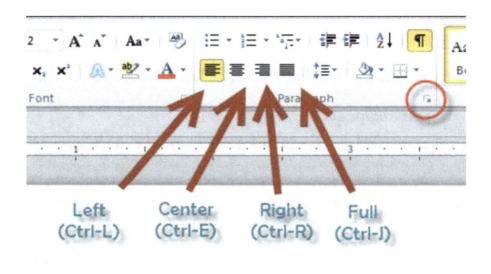

Creating Bulleted and Numbered Lists

1. **Bulleted Lists**:
   - o To create a bulleted list:
     1. Select the text or list of items you want to turn into a bulleted list.
     2. In the **Paragraph** group on the **Home** tab, click the **Bullets** button (the bullet point icon).

3. You can customize the bullet style by clicking the small arrow next to the **Bullets** button and selecting **Define New Bullet**. This allows you to choose symbols, pictures, or custom bullet styles.

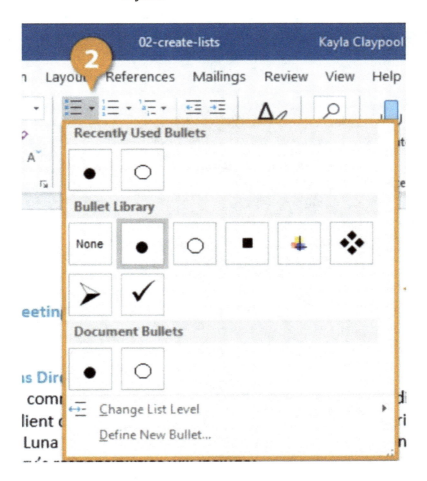

2. **Numbered Lists**:
   o To create a numbered list:

1. Select the text or list of items you want to turn into a numbered list.
2. In the **Paragraph** group, click the **Numbering** button (the numbered list icon).
3. To customize the numbering style, click the small arrow next to the **Numbering** button and choose from different number formats (such as **1, 2, 3, i, ii, iii**, or **A, B, C**).

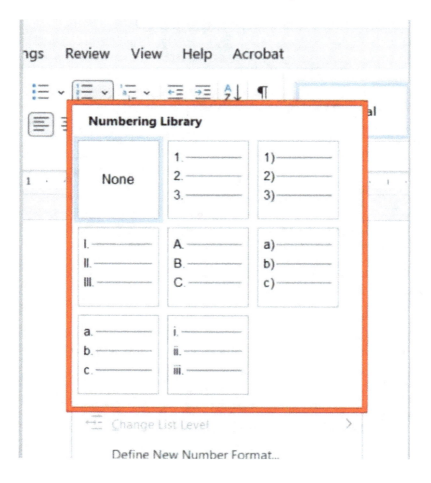

3. **Multi-Level Lists**:
    - To create a multi-level list (a nested list with indents):
        1. Use the **Tab** key on your keyboard to indent an item within a list.
        2. Use **Shift + Tab** to reduce the indentation level. This allows you to create a hierarchical structure within the list.
4. **Adjusting List Styles**:
    - You can change the list's bullet or numbering style, font, or indentation by using the **Paragraph Settings** or selecting **Define New Number Format** under the **Numbering** options.

Adding Borders and Shading to Paragraphs

1. **Adding Borders**:
    - Borders can help emphasize specific paragraphs or separate sections in your document.
        1. Select the paragraph or paragraphs where you want to add a border.
        2. Go to the **Design** tab and click on the **Borders** button in the **Page Background** group.
        3. From the dropdown menu, select options like **Bottom Border**, **Top Border**, **All Borders**, etc.
        4. For more detailed border options, select **Borders and Shading** from the dropdown. This opens a dialog box where you can choose line styles, color, and width.
2. **Adding Shading**:

- Shading adds color to the background of your paragraph, helping it stand out.
  1. Select the paragraph where you want to add shading.
  2. Go to the **Design** tab and click on **Shading** in the **Page Background** group.
  3. Choose a color from the palette or click **More Colors** to select a custom color.
  4. You can adjust shading to apply to the entire paragraph or just part of the paragraph using the **Borders and Shading** dialog box.

3. **Combining Borders and Shading**:
   - You can apply both a border and shading to a paragraph simultaneously to highlight important content.
     1. Select the paragraph.
     2. Go to **Home > Paragraph > Borders**, and choose **Borders and Shading** for detailed options.
     3. In the dialog box, select both the **Borders** and **Shading** tabs to adjust the border and shading to your preferences.

Chapter 5. Page Layout and Design Basics

Setting Page Margins, Orientation, and Size

1. **Page Margins**:
   - Margins are the blank space around the edges of your document. You can set custom margins to control the layout of your content.
     1. Go to the **Layout** tab.
     2. In the **Page Setup** group, click on **Margins**.
     3. Choose from predefined margin options like **Normal**, **Narrow**, **Wide**, or select **Custom Margins** to specify your own values for top, bottom, left, and right margins.

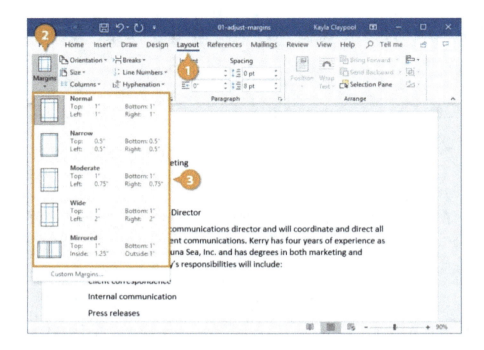

4. In the **Custom Margins** window, you can also adjust the **Gutter**, which adds extra space for binding, and select the **Multiple Pages** option if needed.

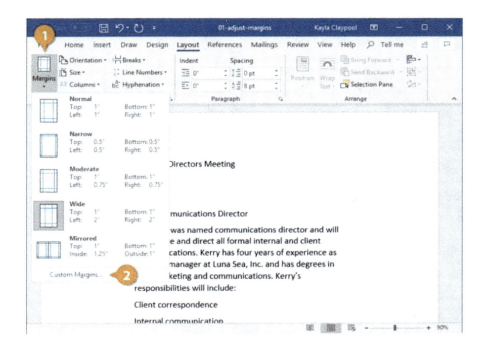

Client correspondence

Internal communication

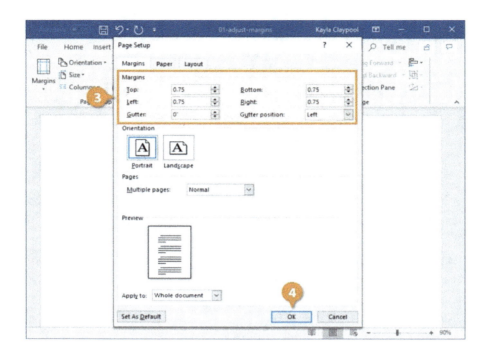

2. **Page Orientation**:
   - ○ **Portrait**: The default orientation with the longer side of the page as the height (vertical).
   - ○ **Landscape**: Rotates the page to have the longer side as the width (horizontal).
       1. To change the orientation, go to the **Layout** tab.
       2. In the **Page Setup** group, click on **Orientation**.
       3. Select **Portrait** or **Landscape**.

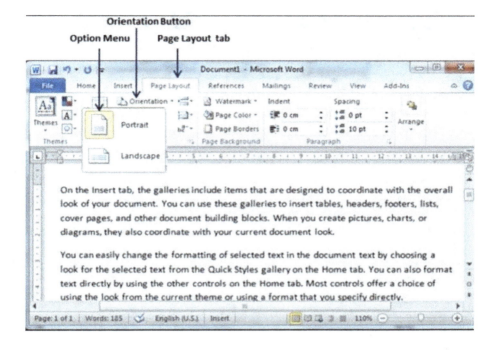

On the Insert tab, the galleries include items that are designed to coordinate with the overall look of your document. You can use these galleries to insert tables, headers, footers, lists, cover pages, and other document building blocks. When you create pictures, charts, or diagrams, they also coordinate with your current document look.

You can easily change the formatting of selected text in the document text by choosing a look for the selected text from the Quick Styles gallery on the Home tab. You can also format text directly by using the other controls on the Home tab. Most controls offer a choice of using the look from the current theme or using a format that you specify directly.

3. **Page Size**:
    o You can adjust the page size based on your needs, such as changing it from **Letter** (8.5" x 11") to **A4** (210mm x 297mm) or custom dimensions.
        1. In the **Layout** tab, click **Size** in the **Page Setup** group.
        2. Choose from standard sizes or click **More Paper Sizes** to enter custom dimensions.

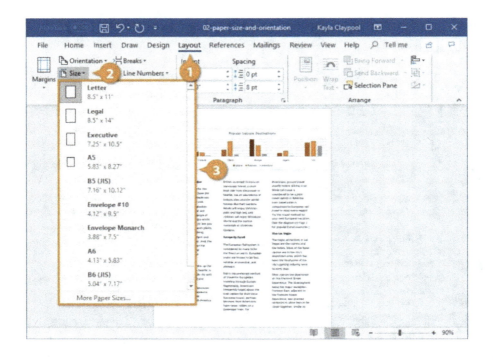

Using Page Breaks and Section Breaks

1. **Page Breaks**:
   - A page break forces the text after it to start on a new page. It is useful when you want to separate sections or chapters of your document.
     1. Place your cursor where you want the page to break.
     2. Go to the **Insert** tab and click on **Page Break** or press **Ctrl + Enter**.

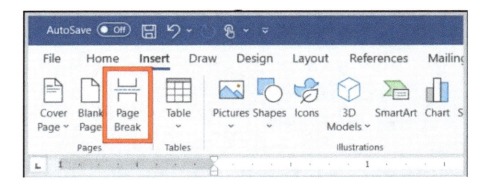

3. This will push the content after the break to a new page.

2. **Section Breaks**:

   o Section breaks divide the document into sections, allowing you to apply different formatting to different parts of the document (e.g., changing headers, footers, or page numbering).

      1. Place your cursor where the section break should occur.

      2. Go to the **Layout** tab, click on **Breaks**, and choose from options like:

         ▪ **Next Page**: Starts a new section on the next page.

         ▪ **Continuous**: Starts a new section on the same page.

         ▪ **Even Page** or **Odd Page**: Starts the new section on the next even or odd page.

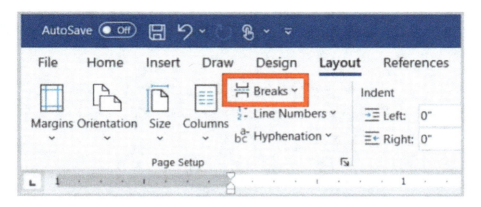

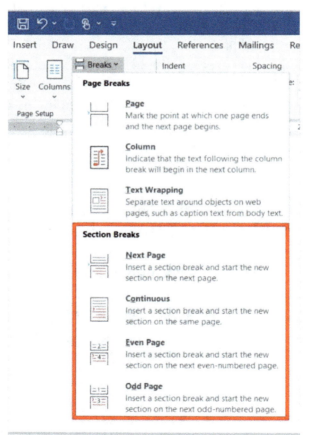

3. Section breaks are helpful when dealing with documents that require different page numbering, headers, or layouts for different sections.

Working with Headers, Footers, and Page Numbers

1. **Headers and Footers**:
   - Headers appear at the top of the page, while footers are at the bottom. These sections can contain information like document titles, author names, or dates.
     1. To add or edit headers and footers, go to the **Insert** tab and select **Header** or **Footer** in the **Header & Footer** group.

     2. Choose a built-in design or select **Edit Header** or **Edit Footer** to customize them.

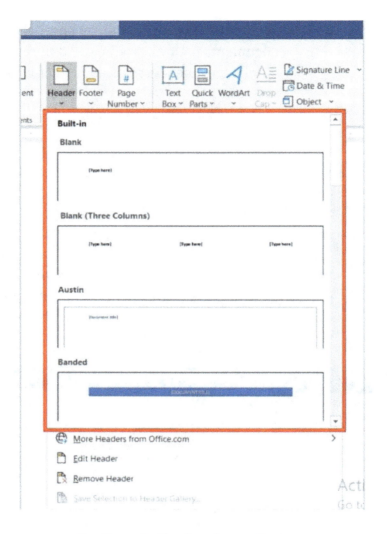

3. Once in the header or footer area, you can add text, images, page numbers, or other elements.

2. **Page Numbers**:
   - Page numbers are often added to the header or footer to indicate the current page in the document.

1. To add page numbers, go to the **Insert** tab and click on **Page Number** in the **Header & Footer** group.

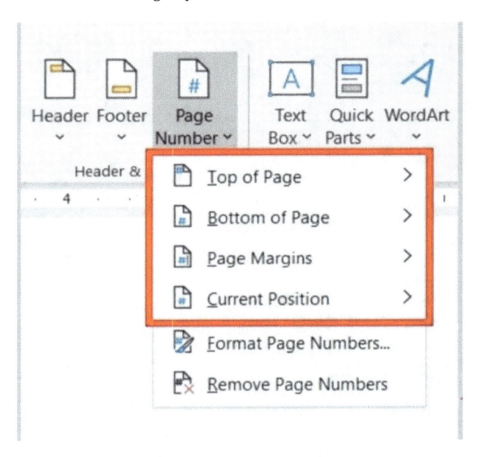

2. Choose the location (top or bottom of the page) and alignment (left, center, right).

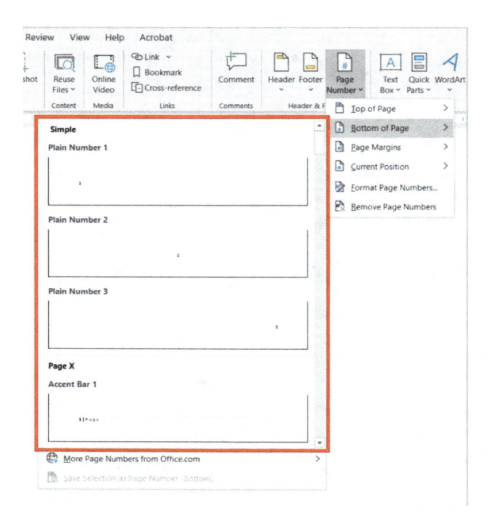

3. You can also format page numbers by selecting **Format Page Numbers** from the dropdown, where you can choose number formats (1, 2, 3 or i, ii, iii) or start the numbering from a specific number.

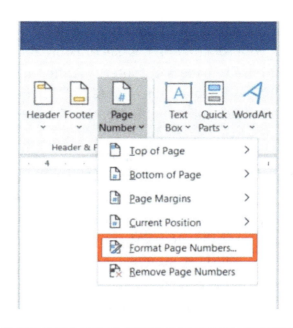

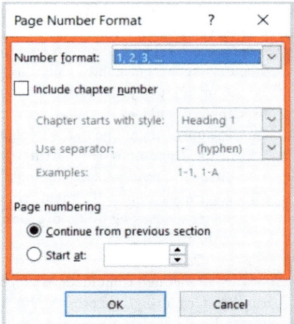

3. **Different Headers and Footers for Different Sections**:
   - If your document has section breaks and you want different headers or footers in different sections (e.g., a different header for Chapter 1), uncheck the **Link to Previous** option in the **Header & Footer Tools** Design tab for that section.
     1. To do this, click on the header or footer in the section you want to change.
     2. In the **Header & Footer Tools**, click **Link to Previous** to deselect it. This breaks the connection between the previous section and the current one.

Applying Themes and Styles

1. **Themes**:
   - A theme is a set of coordinated colors, fonts, and effects that you can apply to your entire document to create a consistent look and feel.
     1. To apply a theme, go to the **Design** tab.
     2. In the **Document Formatting** group, select a theme from the available options.
     3. You can customize the theme colors, fonts, and effects by clicking on **Colors**, **Fonts**, or **Effects** in the **Design** tab.
2. **Styles**:
   - Styles are predefined combinations of font formatting, paragraph formatting, and other settings that you can apply to headings, body text, and other parts of the

document. Using styles helps maintain consistency in formatting.

1. To apply a style, go to the **Home** tab and locate the **Styles** group.
2. Click on a style like **Heading 1**, **Heading 2**, or **Normal** to apply it to your text.
3. You can modify a style by right-clicking the style and selecting **Modify**, where you can change the font, size, color, and other formatting options.
4. You can also create custom styles by selecting **New Style** from the **Styles** group.

Chapter 6. Working with Tables

Creating and Formatting Tables

1. **Creating a Table**:
   - You can quickly insert a table by using the **Insert** tab.
     1. Go to the **Insert** tab in the Ribbon.
     2. In the **Tables** group, click **Table**.

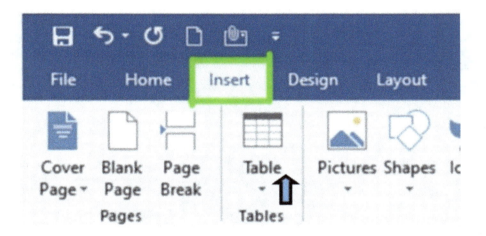

3. Select the number of rows and columns you want by hovering over the grid in the dropdown menu, or click **Insert Table** for more customization.

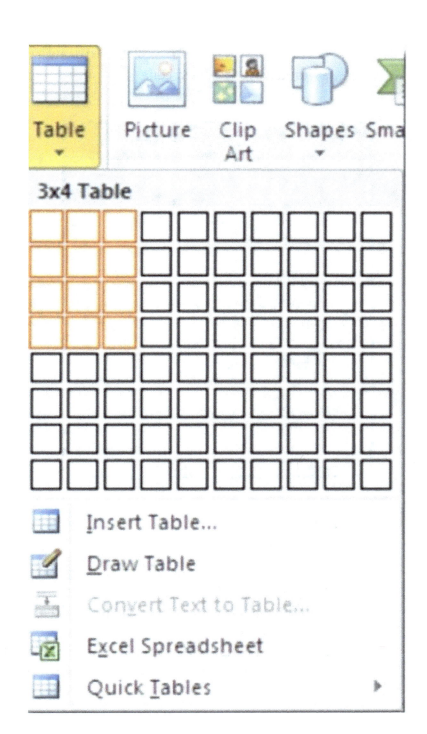

4. You can also click **Draw Table** to draw a custom table with freeform cells.

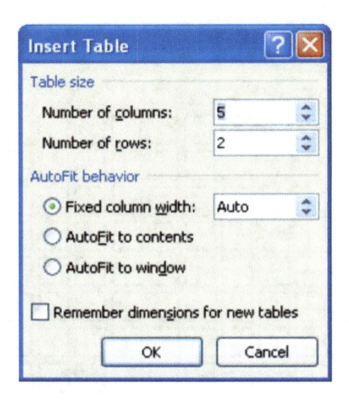

2. **Formatting Tables**:
   o Once a table is inserted, you can apply a variety of formatting options to enhance its appearance.
      1. Click anywhere inside the table to reveal the **Table Tools** tab, which includes **Design** and **Layout** tabs.
      2. On the **Design** tab, you can choose from built-in table styles that automatically format the table

with alternating row colors, borders, and text formatting.

3. You can also customize the table style by clicking on **Shading** to change the background color of cells and **Borders** to adjust cell borders (color, thickness, etc.).

4. Use **Table Styles** in the **Table Tools Design** tab to quickly apply consistent formatting to your table.

Inserting, Deleting, and Merging Cells, Rows, and Columns

1. **Inserting Cells, Rows, or Columns**:
   - To insert additional content in your table:
     1. **Insert a Row**:
        - Right-click on a row where you want to add a new one.
        - Select **Insert** and choose **Insert Rows Above** or **Insert Rows Below** depending on where you want the new row.
     2. **Insert a Column**:
        - Right-click on a column where you want to add a new one.
        - Select **Insert** and choose **Insert Columns to the Left** or **Insert Columns to the Right**.

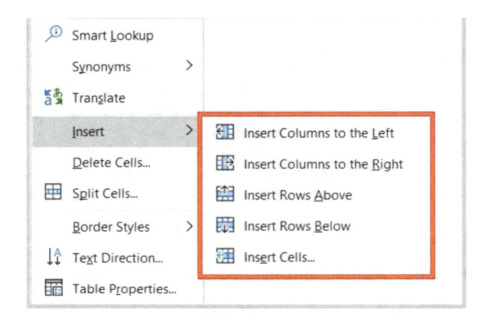

2. **Deleting Cells, Rows, or Columns**:
   - If you no longer need specific rows or columns:
     1. Select the row or column by clicking on the row number or column letter.
     2. Right-click and select **Delete** from the context menu.
     3. You can choose to delete the **Entire Row** or **Entire Column** or just **Delete Cells** (which lets you choose to shift cells left or up).
3. **Merging Cells**:
   - Merging cells allows you to combine two or more adjacent cells into a single cell (useful for headings or titles).
     1. Select the cells you want to merge.
     2. On the **Layout** tab under **Table Tools**, click on **Merge Cells** in the **Merge** group.

3. The selected cells will merge into one, expanding to fill the area.

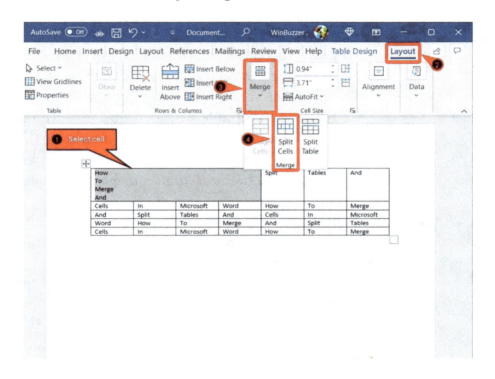

o You can unmerge cells by selecting the merged cell and clicking **Split Cells** under the **Layout** tab, where you can specify the number of columns or rows to split into.

Adjusting Table Alignment and Text Wrapping

1. **Adjusting Table Alignment**:
   o You can align your table within the page to change its overall position.

1. Click anywhere in the table.
2. On the **Layout** tab, in the **Table** group, use the **Properties** button to open the **Table Properties** dialog box.
3. Under the **Table** tab, you can choose to align the table **Left**, **Center**, or **Right** within the page.
4. Under the **Text Wrapping** options, you can choose **None** (table will not wrap text around it), **Around** (text will wrap around the table), or **Through** (allows the text to flow around and through the table, useful for images or complex designs).

2. **Adjusting Text Wrapping Within Cells**:
   o Inside the cells of the table, you can adjust text wrapping to control how text fits in each cell.
      1. Select the cell or cells where you want to adjust the text wrapping.
      2. Right-click and choose **Table Properties**.
      3. In the **Cell** tab, under **Text Wrapping**, choose whether the text should be wrapped within the cell or overflow outside the cell if the content exceeds the available space.

3. **Cell Alignment**:
   o You can align text within individual cells to adjust the position of text horizontally or vertically.
      1. Select the cell or group of cells you want to adjust.
      2. On the **Layout** tab, you will find options for **Align Left**, **Center**, **Align Right**, and vertical alignment (top, middle, bottom) in the **Alignment** group.

3. Adjusting the alignment of text within cells helps improve readability, especially in tables that contain varied content.

Chapter 7. Inserting Objects and Media

Adding Pictures, Shapes, Icons, and SmartArt

1. **Adding Pictures**:
    - Pictures can add visual appeal and clarity to your document.
        1. Go to the **Insert** tab.
        2. In the **Illustrations** group, click on **Pictures**.
        3. You can choose **This Device** to insert an image from your computer, or **Online Pictures** to find images on the web (via Bing or OneDrive).

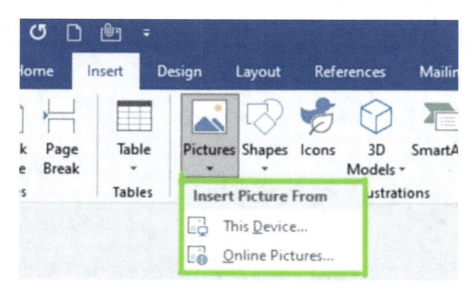

4. Select the image file you want to insert, and click **Insert**.

5. Once inserted, you can resize the image, crop it, or apply picture styles from the **Picture Tools** tab that appears when the image is selected.

2. **Adding Shapes**:

  o You can insert various shapes such as rectangles, circles, arrows, and lines to highlight certain content.

     1. Go to the **Insert** tab.

     2. Click on **Shapes** in the **Illustrations** group.

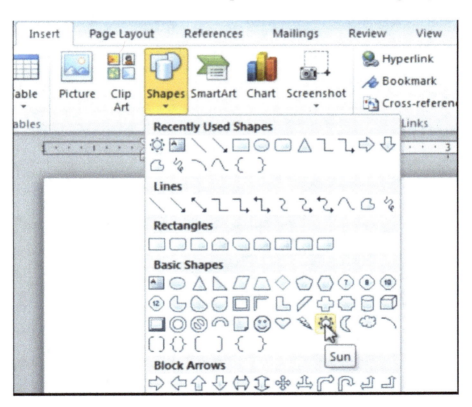

3. Select the desired shape from the dropdown menu.
4. Click and drag your mouse on the document to draw the shape.
5. Use the **Format** tab (which appears once the shape is selected) to customize the shape's fill color, outline, and effects.

3. **Adding Icons**:
   o Icons can help represent ideas or sections visually.
      1. Go to the **Insert** tab.
      2. In the **Illustrations** group, click **Icons**.
      3. A library of icons will appear, categorized by themes such as people, arrows, and more.

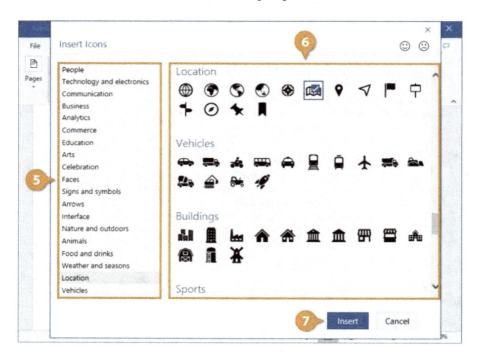

4. Choose an icon and click **Insert** to add it to your document.
5. You can resize and change the color of the icon using the **Format** tab.

4. **Adding SmartArt**:
   - SmartArt graphics allow you to create professional-looking diagrams such as lists, processes, cycles, and hierarchies.
     1. Go to the **Insert** tab.
     2. Click **SmartArt** in the **Illustrations** group.

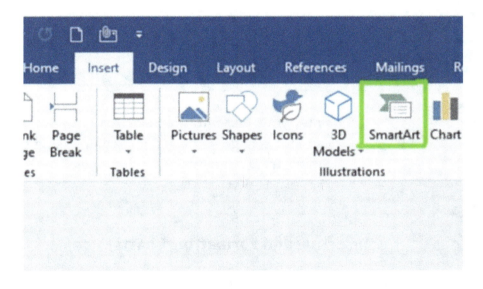

3. Choose a SmartArt graphic type (e.g., List, Process, Cycle, Hierarchy).
4. Click on the graphic style you prefer, and click **OK**.

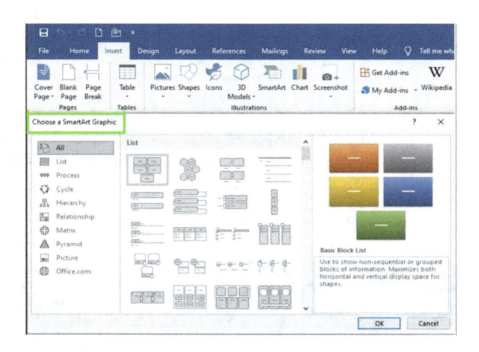

5. Enter your text into the SmartArt graphic. You can also change its design and colors using the **SmartArt Design** tab.

Inserting and Formatting Charts

1. **Inserting Charts**:
   - Charts allow you to visually represent data in a structured and easy-to-understand format.
     1. Go to the **Insert** tab.
     2. In the **Illustrations** group, click on **Chart**.
     3. Choose the type of chart you want (e.g., Bar, Line, Pie, Column).

4. A default chart will appear, and a data spreadsheet will open, allowing you to input your data.
5. Once you've entered your data, click **Close** to return to the document.

2. **Formatting Charts**:
   o After inserting a chart, you can customize its appearance:
      1. Click on the chart to activate the **Chart Tools** tab, which includes the **Design** and **Format** options.
      2. Under **Design**, you can switch chart styles, select a different chart layout, or change the color scheme.
      3. Under **Format**, you can adjust the chart elements such as the title, legend, data labels, and axes. You can also adjust the size of the chart.

3. **Modifying Data in Charts**:
   o To update the data in your chart, you can simply click on the chart, then click **Edit Data** to modify the spreadsheet.
      ▪ This will open the Excel-like data editor where you can change the numbers and categories displayed in the chart.
   o As you make changes to the data, the chart will automatically update to reflect those changes.

Embedding and Linking Excel Data

1. **Embedding Excel Data**:
   - Embedding an Excel worksheet in Word allows you to insert a table or spreadsheet directly into your document.
     1. Place your cursor where you want the Excel data to appear.
     2. Go to the **Insert** tab and click on **Table**.
     3. Choose **Excel Spreadsheet** from the options.
     4. A new Excel sheet will appear where you can enter data.
     5. Once done, click outside the embedded Excel data to return to Word.
   - The data is embedded as part of the Word document, so you can edit it directly within Word, and it will remain static unless manually updated.
2. **Linking Excel Data**:
   - If you want the Excel data to be updated automatically whenever the source file is changed, you can link the Excel data to Word.
     1. First, select and copy the data from your Excel file.
     2. In Word, place your cursor where you want the data to appear.
     3. Go to the **Home** tab, click the **Paste** dropdown, and select **Paste Special**.
     4. In the dialog box, select **Paste Link** and choose **Microsoft Excel Worksheet Object**.

5. The data will appear as a linked object, and any updates in the Excel file will automatically update in the Word document.

o This allows you to maintain dynamic content that is always up-to-date without having to manually re-enter data in Word.

Chapter 8. Proofing and Reviewing Documents

Using Spell Check, Grammar Check, and Thesaurus

1. **Spell Check**:
   - **Microsoft Word** has a built-in spell checker that automatically highlights misspelled words as you type.
     1. To manually run a spell check, go to the **Review** tab.
     2. In the **Proofing** group, click **Spelling & Grammar**.
     3. Word will scan the document and suggest corrections. You can choose to **Change** a suggestion, **Ignore** it, or **Add** it to your dictionary.
   - **Auto-correct** can also automatically fix common typos as you type. You can customize the Auto-correct settings by going to **File > Options > Proofing > AutoCorrect Options**.
2. **Grammar Check**:
   - In addition to spelling errors, Word can also detect grammatical issues like sentence fragments, comma splices, and subject-verb agreement.
     1. Grammar check is automatically included with the spell check.

2. When you run the **Spelling & Grammar** check, Word will highlight grammatical issues with a green squiggly line and suggest corrections.
3. Review each suggestion and apply the appropriate fixes.

3. **Thesaurus**:
   - The **Thesaurus** helps you find synonyms for words to enhance your writing or avoid repetition.
     1. Right-click on any word and select **Synonyms**.
     2. A list of synonyms will appear, and you can choose an alternative word from the list.
     3. Alternatively, select a word, go to the **Review** tab, and click **Thesaurus** in the **Proofing** group to open the Thesaurus pane.

Adding Comments and Using Track Changes

1. **Adding Comments**:
   - Comments are useful for providing feedback or notes within a document without changing the actual text.
     1. Select the text or place your cursor where you want to add a comment.
     2. Go to the **Review** tab and click **New Comment** in the **Comments** group.

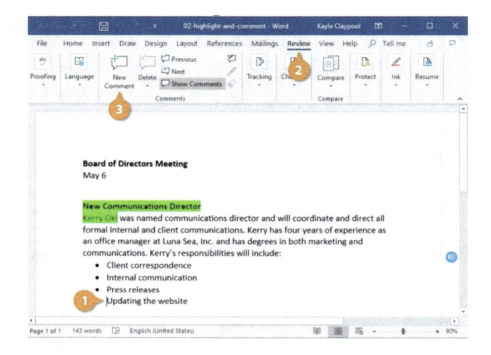

3. A comment bubble will appear in the margin where you can type your comment.

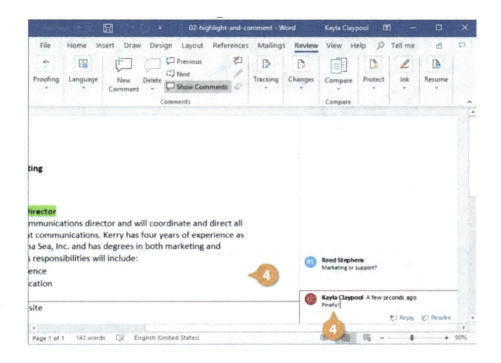

4. To edit or delete a comment, right-click the comment bubble and choose the appropriate option.

2. **Track Changes**:

   o **Track Changes** allows you to make edits to a document while keeping a record of changes. This is particularly useful for collaboration.

      1. Go to the **Review** tab.
      2. In the **Tracking** group, click **Track Changes** to enable the feature. Once enabled, any changes you make (inserting, deleting, or formatting text) will be tracked.

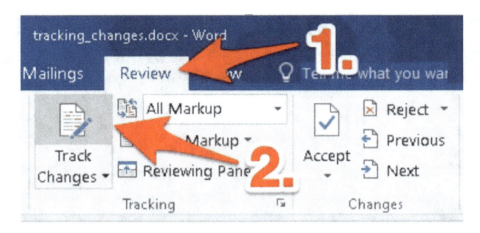

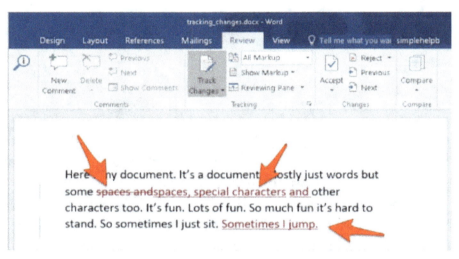

3. To view the changes, you can toggle between **Final** and **Final Showing Markup** views from the **Review** tab.

4. To accept or reject changes, click **Accept** or **Reject** in the **Changes** group on the **Review** tab.

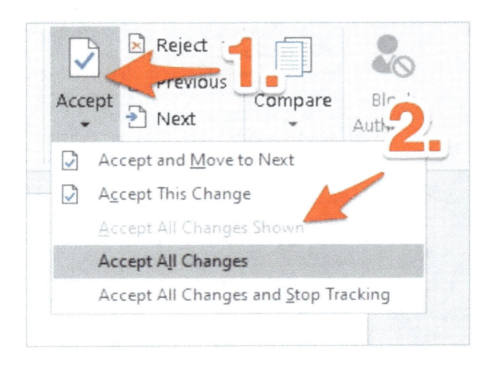

5. You can also customize how the changes are displayed (e.g., colors, underlining) in the **Track Changes Options** under **Review > Tracking**.

Comparing and Combining Documents

1. **Comparing Documents**:
   o When working with multiple versions of a document, you can compare the differences between two versions to see what has changed.
      1. Go to the **Review** tab.

2. In the **Compare** group, click **Compare** and select **Compare...** from the dropdown.
3. In the **Compare Documents** dialog, select the two documents you want to compare (the original and the revised document).
4. Word will show a comparison, highlighting any changes in the document, such as text added, deleted, or modified.

2. **Combining Documents**:
   o **Combining** documents merges two versions into a single document while preserving all changes, comments, and tracked edits.
     1. Go to the **Review** tab.
     2. In the **Compare** group, click **Combine** and select **Combine...** from the dropdown.
     3. In the **Combine Documents** dialog, select the original and revised documents.
     4. Word will merge the documents and show all changes, making it easy to finalize the document.

Chapter 9. Using Advanced Features

Introduction to Mail Merge

1. **What is Mail Merge?**
   - **Mail Merge** is a tool in Microsoft Word that allows you to create personalized documents, such as letters, envelopes, and labels, by merging a data source (usually an Excel spreadsheet or Access database) with a template document.
2. **Creating Letters Using Mail Merge:**
   - **Step 1**: Open a new or existing Word document where you want to insert personalized information (e.g., name, address).
   - **Step 2**: Go to the **Mailings** tab on the ribbon and click **Start Mail Merge**. Select **Letters** as your document type.

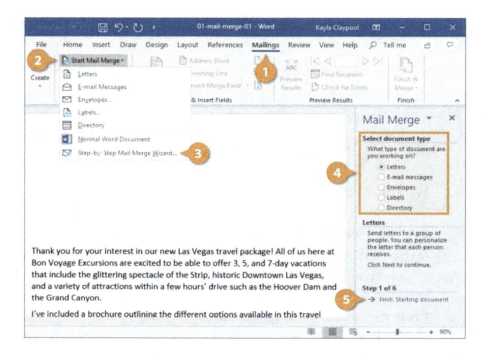

- o **Step 3**: Click **Select Recipients** and choose **Use an Existing List** to connect to your data source (such as an Excel spreadsheet).

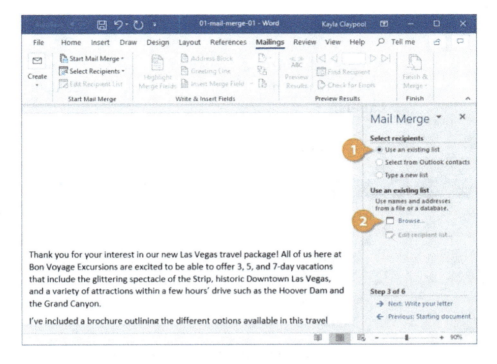

- o **Step 4**: Insert merge fields (such as Name, Address, etc.) by clicking **Insert Merge Field**. Select the field that matches your data.
- o **Step 5**: Complete the letter template, and then click **Finish & Merge** to either print the letters, create a new document, or send them via email.
3. **Creating Envelopes and Labels Using Mail Merge**:
   - o **Envelopes**:
     1. Go to the **Mailings** tab and select **Start Mail Merge**, then choose **Envelopes**.
     2. Specify the envelope size and customize the layout.
     3. Click **Select Recipients** and choose your data source.

4. Insert the merge fields into the envelope template.
5. Click **Finish & Merge** to print the envelopes or create a new document with the merged data.

○ **Labels**:
1. Go to the **Mailings** tab and select **Start Mail Merge**, then choose **Labels**.

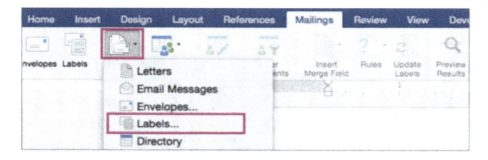

2. Select the type of label you want to use (e.g., Avery labels).

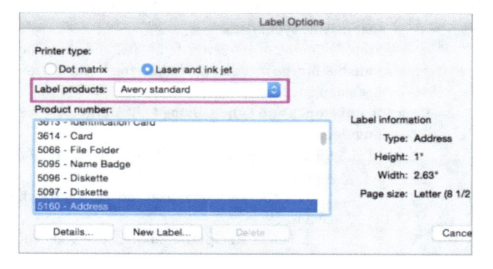

3. Insert the merge fields (like Name and Address) into the label template.
4. Click **Finish & Merge** to print the labels.

Creating and Using Bookmarks and Cross-References

1. **Bookmarks**:
   - **What are Bookmarks?**
     - A **Bookmark** is a placeholder in your document that allows you to link to specific locations within the same document. You can use bookmarks to navigate easily or link text from elsewhere in the document to specific sections.
   - **Creating Bookmarks**:
     1. Select the text or location where you want to create a bookmark.
     2. Go to the **Insert** tab, and in the **Links** group, click **Bookmark**.
     3. In the dialog box, type a name for the bookmark and click **Add**.
   - **Linking to Bookmarks**:
     0. Highlight the text you want to turn into a hyperlink.
     1. Go to the **Insert** tab, click **Link**, and select **Place in This Document**.
     2. Choose the bookmark name you want to link to and click **OK**.
2. **Cross-References**:
   - **What are Cross-References?**

- A **Cross-Reference** is a link that refers to other parts of your document, like headings, figures, or tables. When the referenced text changes, the cross-reference automatically updates to reflect that change.
  - **Inserting Cross-References**:
    0. Place the cursor where you want to insert the cross-reference.
    1. Go to the **References** tab, click **Cross-reference** in the **Captions** group.
    2. In the dialog box, choose the type of item you want to refer to (e.g., headings, figures, tables).
    3. Select the specific item to reference and choose how it should appear (e.g., hyperlink, text only).
    4. Click **Insert** to add the cross-reference to your document.

Generating a Table of Contents and Index

1. **Table of Contents (TOC)**:
   - **What is a Table of Contents?**
     - A **Table of Contents (TOC)** is a list of headings and subheadings in your document with links that allow readers to jump directly to specific sections.
   - **Creating a TOC**:
     1. First, ensure that you have used **Heading Styles** (e.g., Heading 1, Heading 2) to format your section titles.

2. Place the cursor where you want the TOC to appear (typically at the beginning of the document).
3. Go to the **References** tab and click **Table of Contents** in the **Table of Contents** group.
4. Choose a style for your TOC (e.g., automatic or manual).
5. Word will generate a TOC based on the heading styles in your document. To update it as you add content, right-click on the TOC and select **Update Field**.

2. **Index**:
   o **What is an Index?**
     ▪ An **Index** is an alphabetical list of key topics and terms in your document, along with page numbers where they appear.
   o **Creating an Index**:
     0. Select the text you want to mark for the index (such as a keyword or phrase).
     1. Go to the **References** tab and click **Mark Entry** in the **Index** group.
     2. In the dialog box, customize the entry (e.g., main entry, subentry) and click **Mark**.
     3. After marking all terms, place the cursor where you want the index to appear.
     4. Click **Insert Index** in the **Index** group.
     5. Choose an index format and click **OK** to insert the index.

Chapter 10. Exporting and Printing Documents

Saving Documents in Different Formats

1. **Saving in Different Formats**:
   o Microsoft Word allows you to save documents in various formats, making them compatible with other software and suitable for different purposes.

Steps to Save in Different Formats:

2. Open the document you want to save.
3. Go to the **File** tab and click **Save As**.
4. Choose the location where you want to save the document (e.g., OneDrive, local folder).
5. In the **Save as type** dropdown menu, select the desired format:
   - **.docx** (default Word format)
   - **.pdf** (Portable Document Format for sharing and printing)
   - **.rtf** (Rich Text Format for compatibility with other word processors)
   - **.txt** (Plain Text without formatting)
   - **.html** (for web documents)
   - **.odt** (OpenDocument Text for use with OpenOffice)

6. After selecting the format, click **Save**.

Setting Up Print Options (Page Range, Duplex Printing, Scaling)

1. **Page Range**:
   - **Page Range** allows you to specify which pages of the document you want to print. You can print all pages, specific pages, or a range of pages.

   Steps to Set Page Range:

   2. Go to the **File** tab and click **Print**.
   3. In the **Print Setup** area, under **Settings**, you will see the **Pages** option.
   4. You can select from:
      - **All Pages** to print the entire document.
      - **Custom Range** where you enter a specific page range (e.g., 1-5, 7, 9-10) to print.
      - **Current Page** to print only the page you are currently viewing.
2. **Duplex Printing**:
   - **Duplex printing** refers to printing on both sides of a page. It helps save paper and can make your printed documents look more professional.

   Steps to Set Duplex Printing:

   1. Go to the **File** tab and click **Print**.

2. Under **Printer**, make sure you select a printer that supports duplex printing.
3. Under **Settings**, you will see an option for **Print on Both Sides**. Select this option if you want to print double-sided.
4. Choose the preferred binding method (e.g., flip on long edge or short edge) depending on how you want the pages oriented.

3. **Scaling**:
   ○ **Scaling** adjusts how content fits on the printed page. You can scale a document to make it fit on fewer pages or adjust it to a specific paper size.

Steps to Set Scaling:

1. Go to the **File** tab and click **Print**.
2. Under **Settings**, look for the **Scale to Paper Size** option.
3. Select a scale option:
   ▪ **No Scaling** (prints as is).
   ▪ **Fit to One Page** (shrinks or enlarges the content to fit a single page).
   ▪ **Custom Scaling** (manually adjust the scale percentage).

Printing a Document

1. **Steps to Print**:
   - **Step 1**: Open your document in Microsoft Word.
   - **Step 2**: Go to the **File** tab and click **Print**.
   - **Step 3**: Choose the printer you want to use from the **Printer** dropdown list.
   - **Step 4**: Adjust your print settings (page range, duplex printing, scaling, color options).
   - **Step 5**: If needed, check the **Preview** to ensure everything looks correct.

- o **Step 6**: Click the **Print** button to send the document to the printer.

Advanced Print Settings:

- o Some printers offer additional settings like selecting print quality (draft, normal, high quality) and paper type (e.g., plain, glossy).
- o If your document contains images or complex formatting, you may want to adjust the print quality to ensure the document looks as expected.

Appendices

Microsoft Word Cheat Sheet

Common Shortcuts and Tips for Productivity

Here are some of the most commonly used **keyboard shortcuts** in Microsoft Word that can help speed up your workflow and improve productivity:

General Shortcuts

- **Ctrl + N**: Create a new document
- **Ctrl + O**: Open an existing document
- **Ctrl + S**: Save the current document
- **Ctrl + P**: Print the document
- **Ctrl + W**: Close the current document
- **Ctrl + F**: Open the Find dialog box
- **Ctrl + H**: Open the Find and Replace dialog box
- **Ctrl + Z**: Undo the last action
- **Ctrl + Y**: Redo the last undone action
- **Ctrl + A**: Select all content in the document
- **Ctrl + C**: Copy selected text or objects
- **Ctrl + X**: Cut selected text or objects
- **Ctrl + V**: Paste copied or cut content

- **Ctrl + B**: Toggle bold formatting
- **Ctrl + I**: Toggle italic formatting
- **Ctrl + U**: Toggle underline formatting
- **Ctrl + E**: Center align text
- **Ctrl + L**: Left align text
- **Ctrl + R**: Right align text
- **Ctrl + J**: Justify text alignment
- **Ctrl + Shift + N**: Apply the Normal style
- **Ctrl + Shift + S**: Open the Styles pane
- **Ctrl + K**: Insert a hyperlink

Formatting Shortcuts

- **Ctrl + T**: Create a hanging indent
- **Ctrl + M**: Increase paragraph indent
- **Ctrl + Shift + M**: Decrease paragraph indent
- **Ctrl + Q**: Remove paragraph formatting (return to Normal style)
- **Ctrl + 1**: Set line spacing to single
- **Ctrl + 2**: Set line spacing to double
- **Ctrl + 5**: Set line spacing to 1.5
- **Ctrl + Shift + L**: Apply a bullet point to the selected text
- **Ctrl + Shift + N**: Apply the Normal paragraph style

Navigation Shortcuts

- **Ctrl + Right Arrow**: Move the cursor one word to the right
- **Ctrl + Left Arrow**: Move the cursor one word to the left

- **Ctrl + Down Arrow**: Move the cursor down one paragraph
- **Ctrl + Up Arrow**: Move the cursor up one paragraph
- **Home**: Move the cursor to the beginning of the current line
- **End**: Move the cursor to the end of the current line
- **Ctrl + Home**: Move the cursor to the beginning of the document
- **Ctrl + End**: Move the cursor to the end of the document
- **Page Up**: Move up one screen
- **Page Down**: Move down one screen

Selection Shortcuts

- **Ctrl + Shift + Right Arrow**: Select one word to the right
- **Ctrl + Shift + Left Arrow**: Select one word to the left
- **Shift + Arrow Keys**: Select text character by character or line by line
- **Ctrl + Shift + Arrow Keys**: Select text by whole words or paragraphs
- **Ctrl + A**: Select all text in the document
- **Shift + Home**: Select from the current cursor position to the beginning of the line
- **Shift + End**: Select from the current cursor position to the end of the line

Miscellaneous Shortcuts

- **Alt + Tab**: Switch between open applications
- **Ctrl + Shift + C**: Copy formatting

- **Ctrl + Shift + V**: Paste formatting
- **Ctrl + F1**: Open or hide the Ribbon
- **F7**: Run the spelling and grammar check
- **Ctrl + Enter**: Insert a page break
- **Ctrl + Shift + >**: Increase font size
- **Ctrl + Shift + <**: Decrease font size

Formatting Text with Styles

- **Ctrl + Shift + S**: Open the Styles pane for quick styling
- **Alt + Shift + S**: Show the Styles task pane

Tips for Increased Productivity in Word

1. **Quick Access Toolbar**:
   - Customize the **Quick Access Toolbar** to add shortcuts to your most-used features for easy access. You can add commands like Save, Undo, Redo, and Print by right-clicking any command in the Ribbon and selecting "Add to Quick Access Toolbar."
2. **Use Templates**:
   - Save time by using **Word Templates** for documents you create frequently (e.g., reports, resumes, newsletters). Templates are pre-designed documents with consistent formatting.
3. **Find and Replace**:

- o Use **Find and Replace** (Ctrl + H) to quickly locate specific text and replace it throughout your document. This can save time when editing long documents.
4. **Use Styles for Consistency**:
   - o Use **Styles** to format text consistently throughout your document. For example, apply heading styles for headings and subheadings, making it easier to generate a Table of Contents.
5. **Keyboard Shortcuts for Formatting**:
   - o Mastering shortcuts for common formatting tasks (e.g., bold, italics, alignment) will make formatting your document much faster.
6. **Autocorrect and AutoText**:
   - o Take advantage of **AutoCorrect** to automatically replace common typing errors, and use **AutoText** to insert frequently used blocks of text with a few keystrokes.
7. **Voice Dictation**:
   - o Use **Dictate** (available in Word 365) to speak your content and have it transcribed into text automatically. This can be useful for drafting long documents quickly.

Glossary of Key Microsoft Word Terminology

Here are definitions for essential **Microsoft Word terminology** to help you navigate the application with confidence:

A

- **Alignment**: Refers to how text is positioned within a document. Common alignments include left, right, center, and justified.
- **AutoCorrect**: A feature that automatically corrects common typing errors, such as replacing "teh" with "the."
- **AutoText**: A feature that allows you to store frequently used text (such as your name or address) and insert it with a shortcut.

B

- **Bookmark**: A feature used to mark specific locations within a document for easy navigation. Useful for long documents.
- **Bullet Points**: A list style using dots or symbols to organize items in a non-sequential list.

C

- **Capitalize Each Word**: A formatting option that capitalizes the first letter of each word in a selected text.
- **Comment**: An annotation added to the document that doesn't affect the text but allows for feedback or additional information.
- **Cut (Ctrl + X)**: Removes the selected text or object and stores it in the clipboard for later pasting.

D

- **Document**: A file created using Microsoft Word, such as a letter, report, or resume.
- **Double Space**: A line spacing setting that places extra space between lines of text, often used in formal documents.
- **Drop Cap**: A large capital letter that appears at the beginning of a paragraph, often used for emphasis in books or articles.

F

- **File Formats**: The specific types of files you can save your Word document as, such as .docx, .pdf, .rtf, and .txt.
- **Footer**: A section at the bottom of a page in Word that may include page numbers, document title, or author name.
- **Font**: The style and appearance of text, such as Arial, Times New Roman, or Calibri.

G

- **Grammarly**: A tool integrated into Word for checking grammar, spelling, and sentence structure.
- **Group (Ribbon)**: A collection of related commands in the Word ribbon that pertain to a specific task, such as the "Font" group for text formatting.

H

- **Header**: A section at the top of a page in Word that can contain information like the title of the document, author, or page number.
- **Highlight**: The action of marking text with a background color, often used to emphasize specific content.

I

- **Indent**: The space before a paragraph or line of text. Indentation can be used to organize or format documents (e.g., first line indent).
- **Insert Tab**: A section of the Ribbon that contains commands for adding elements to a document, such as images, shapes, and tables.
- **Italic (Ctrl + I)**: A text formatting style where text slants to the right, often used for emphasis or titles.

M

- **Mail Merge**: A feature that allows you to create personalized letters, envelopes, and labels using data from an external source, like an Excel file.
- **Margins**: The blank space around the edges of a page. You can adjust margins for page formatting.

- **Master Document**: A main document that links to other documents, often used for large projects like books or reports.

P

- **Page Break**: An invisible marker that forces Word to start a new page at a specific point in the document.
- **Paragraph**: A block of text with its own formatting settings (e.g., spacing, indentation). It can contain multiple sentences or even just one.
- **Paste (Ctrl + V)**: The action of inserting content that has been cut or copied into a new location in the document.

S

- **Section Break**: A break that divides a document into sections, allowing different page layouts, headers, and footers within the same document.
- **Styles**: A predefined set of formatting options that can be applied to text (such as headings or body text) to ensure consistency throughout the document.
- **Spell Check (F7)**: A feature that automatically checks the document for spelling errors.

T

- **Track Changes**: A feature that allows you to keep a record of edits and revisions made to a document, useful for collaboration and review.
- **Table of Contents (TOC)**: A list of document sections and headings, usually placed at the beginning of a document. It helps readers navigate the document easily.

W

- **Watermark**: A text or image placed behind the main text of a document, typically used to indicate document status (e.g., "Confidential").
- **Wrap Text**: A setting that determines how text behaves around images or other objects in a document (e.g., text can flow around an image or sit above or below it).

Practice Projects for Microsoft Word

Here are some **practice projects** to help you apply what you've learned in Word:

1. Create a Resume

- **Goal**: Design a professional resume using Word's formatting and layout tools.
- **Key Skills**:
  - Using templates
  - Formatting headings and text

- o Aligning text
- o Inserting bullet points for lists
- **Tips**:
  - o Use Word's resume templates to get started.
  - o Make use of headings for each section (e.g., Education, Experience, Skills).
  - o Bold section headers for clarity.

---

2. Design a Flyer

- **Goal**: Create an eye-catching flyer to promote an event or product.
- **Key Skills**:
  - o Inserting images and shapes
  - o Formatting text with different styles and colors
  - o Using text boxes and WordArt
- **Tips**:
  - o Select a flyer template from Word's design options.
  - o Use high-quality images and creative fonts.
  - o Keep the layout clean and organized, focusing on key points.

---

3. Write a Report

- **Goal**: Draft a professional report with headings, subheadings, and tables.
- **Key Skills**:
  - o Creating a Table of Contents (TOC)

- o   Inserting tables and charts
- o   Using the header and footer sections
- o   Applying styles for consistent formatting
- **Tips**:
  - o   Start with a clear title page.
  - o   Use the Heading styles to organize sections of your report.
  - o   Insert charts or graphs to visualize data.

Index